DATE DUE			
JY 6 '92			
JA 30 '93			
JAN 5 1993			

I·N·S·I·D·E

UNITED STATES

Ian James

Franklin Watts

London · New York · Sydney · Toronto

CONTENTS

© 1990 Franklin Watts
96 Leonard Street
London EC2 4HA

Franklin Watts Inc.
387 Park Avenue South
New York, N.Y. 10016

Franklin Watts Australia
14 Mars Road
Lane Cove
NSW 2066

Design: K & Co
Illustrations: Hayward Art Group

UK ISBN: 0 7496 0064 0
US ISBN: 0-531-14029-6
Library of Congress Catalog
Card Number: 89-38984

Phototypeset by Lineage Ltd,
Watford

Printed in Belgium

Front cover: ZEFA
Back cover: ZEFA
Frontispiece: Hutchison Library

Additional pictures: Chapel Studios
Picture Library 14; Chris Fairclough
11B, 15, 16T, 17, 18T, 18B, 19, 20, 24B,
30; Michael Holford 7; Hutchison
Library 4, 5B, 10, 12, 16B, 23, 24T, 25,
28; Kobal Collection 22; Keith Lye 11T,
13; Peter Newark's Pictures 8T, 8B;
Poppertoto 9; Rex Features 21, 29;
ZEFA 5T, 6, 27.

The land

The United States is the world's fourth largest country in both area and population. It is divided into 50 states and the District of Columbia, an area which encloses the capital, Washington D.C. Forty-eight states lie between Canada and Mexico. Alaska, in the northeast corner of North America, was purchased from Russia in 1867. The state of Hawaii is a group of volcanic islands in the central Pacific Ocean. Alaska and Hawaii became states in 1959.

Coastal plains border the east and southeast coasts of mainland United States. Even larger plains, called prairies, lie west of the Appalachian Mountains in the eastern United States.

Below: **The Rocky Mountains are the largest mountain range in North America. It is a region of great scenic beauty.**

4

Above: **Grassy prairies covered the central plains of the United States. Much of the land is now used for growing crops or grazing livestock.**

Left: **The Mississippi is the longest river in the United States. With its tributaries, it drains most of the plains between the Appalachian and Rocky mountains.**

The prairies extend to the Rocky Mountains, the country's largest mountain range. But Alaska contains the country's highest peak, Mount McKinley. Other ranges and high plateaus lie between the Rocky Mountains and the Pacific Ocean.

The northwestern states of Washington and Oregon have a wet, cool climate, while the southwestern coast has a Mediterranean-type climate. Much of the southwestern interior is desert. The interior plains east of the Rockies are dry, but the northeastern coasts have a cool, moist climate. The southeast is subtropical. Florida has many sunny resorts.

Above: **Northern Alaska is a cold and snowy place. But southern Alaska has a mild climate.**

The people and their history

When Christopher Columbus reached the West Indies in 1492, North America contained about 1 million American Indians.

Spanish, English and French pioneers explored North America. From 1607, England founded settlements in the east. By 1760, 13 British colonies had been set up. In the Revolutionary War (1775-1783), these colonies broke away from Britain. They founded a new nation, the United States, on 4 July 1776.

Left: **An artist named John White painted this scene of American Indians fishing in 1587.**

The manner of their fishing.

Above: **The first president of the United States was George Washington. The picture shows him accepting the country's Constitution in 1787.**

Left: **Slave traders shipped about 12 million slaves from Africa to the Americas. Many died on the way. Survivors were forced to work on farms in North and South America.**

In the 19th century, the United States grew rapidly in size. In the west, pioneers fought against the American Indians. In the southeast, there were many slaves who had been brought from Africa. But slavery was ended by the 1861-1865 Civil War.

In the late 19th century, the United States became a great industrial nation. Immigrants arrived from all parts of Europe seeking freedom and new opportunties. Others came from Asia. Today, the United States is a world superpower. About 83 percent of the people are of European descent, and 12 percent are blacks. Other groups include American Indians, Chinese, Japanese, Filipinos, Mexicans, Cubans and Puerto Ricans.

Below: **American troops fought alongside the Allies in World Wars I and II. By 1945, the United States had become one of the world's superpowers. The other superpower is the Soviet Union.**

Towns and cities

In 1790, shortly after the creation of the United States, about 95 percent of the people lived in country areas. But today, only 26 percent live in rural areas. The rest live in cities and towns.

Washington D.C., the country's capital, has a population of 620,000. In the heart of Washington D.C. are many beautiful government buildings. But some suburbs contain overcrowded slums.

The country's most densely populated region runs from Boston, Massachusetts, to Richmond, Virginia, and includes New York City. The next most densely populated regions are Los Angeles-Long Beach in California, and Chicago, Illinois.

Below: **In some states, such as Montana, many people still live in rural communities or on farms or ranches.**

Above: **The Hollywood Bowl, Los Angeles, is famous for its open air concerts.**

Right: **The White House in Washington DC is the home and office of the President of the United States.**

New York City was founded by Dutch traders in 1624. In 1626, the Dutch bought Manhattan Island from local Indians for goods worth $24. Manhattan is now one of the city's five boroughs. Its tall skyscrapers give it a dramatic skyline. New York City is the country's leading transportation, communications, financial and cultural city.

Los Angeles, on the Pacific coast, is a major manufacturing city, famous for its film making industry which grew up in Hollywood. Chicago (nicknamed the "Windy City"), stands on Lake Michigan. It is a major industrial city and port.

Below: **Chicago, the third largest city in the United States, has a beautiful shoreline on Lake Michigan.**

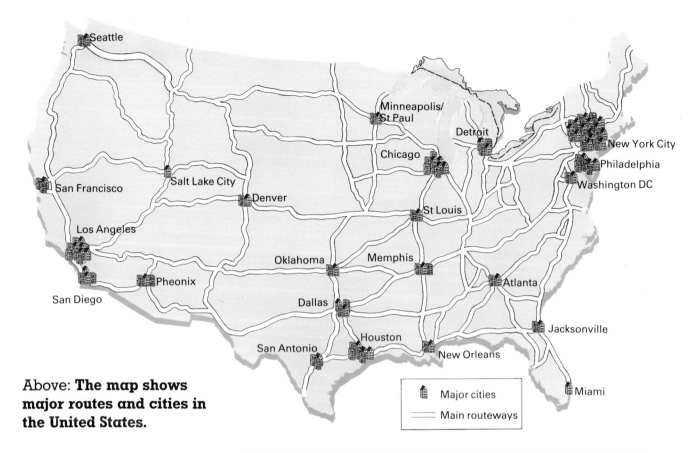

Above: **The map shows major routes and cities in the United States.**

Major cities

Main routeways

Right: **The Statue of Liberty is a symbol of freedom. In the distance are the skyscrapers around Battery Park at the southern tip of Manhattan Island in New York City.**

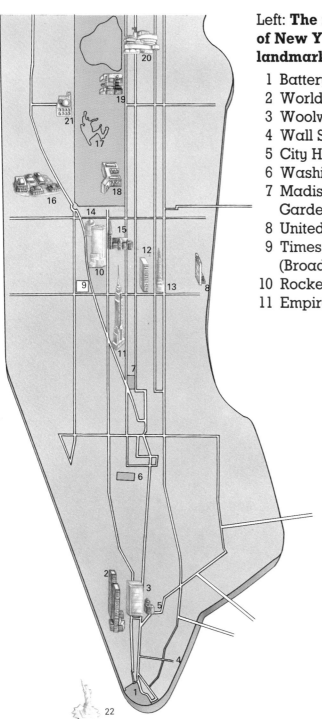

Left: **The map shows some of New York City's landmarks.**

1 Battery Park
2 World Trade Center
3 Woolworth Building
4 Wall Street
5 City Hall
6 Washington Square
7 Madison Square Gardens
8 United Nations Building
9 Times Square (Broadway)
10 Rockefeller Center
11 Empire State Building
12 Pan Am Building
13 Chrysler Building
14 Carnegie Hall
15 St Patrick's Cathedral
16 Lincoln Center
17 Central Park
18 Zoo in Central Park
19 Metropolitan Museum of Art
20 Guggenheim Museum
21 Museum of Natural History
22 Statue of Liberty

Right: **Central Park covers 340 hectares (840 acres) of Manhattan Island.**

Family life

Above: **Pleasant single-family houses with large gardens are found in city suburbs.**

Some families, including many in old inner-city areas, are classed as poor. But on average, American families are among the world's most prosperous. Most city families live in comfortable apartments or in single-family houses. About two-thirds of families own their home. Most have a television and four out of every five own a car. Most homes contain many time-saving devices.

Most households consist only of parents and their children. Other relatives, including grandparents, often live far away. This is because American families often move home, in search of work or better jobs. On average, Americans relocate 10 times in their lifetime.

Above: **Most families live in comfortable modern homes.**

Left: **Many city families travel to country areas for day or weekend trips.**

Food

American cooking is extremely varied. Many regional dishes are well known. They include Boston-baked beans, Southern fried chicken and chili con carne. Families often prepare elaborate meals for special occasions. For example, on Thanksgiving Day, on the fourth Thursday in November, many families enjoy a turkey dinner with pumpkin pie. They are celebrating the first Thanksgiving Day held by the Pilgrims (early colonists) after their first harvest in New England in 1621.

The United States is famous throughout the world for its inexpensive fast food chains, which sell such things as hamburgers, pizzas and apple pie. Many restaurants serve international food. Chinese, French, Italian and Mexican dishes are especially popular.

Below: **Most families buy food in supermarkets.**

Left: **On warm evenings, families often entertain their friends by having a barbecue in the garden.**

Below: **Many Americans enjoy a large breakfast.**

Sports and pastimes

To keep fit, many Americans take part in such sports as cycling, jogging, boating, fishing, golf, skiing, swimming and tennis.

One of the four leading team sports is football, which developed from English rugby. Ice hockey, an extremely fast game, is a leading winter sport. Basketball, another major team sport, was invented in the United States in 1891. Baseball developed in the eastern United States in the mid-19th century from the English game of rounders. Baseball is so popular that it is often called the "national pastime". Many people follow professional football, hockey, basketball and baseball teams on television.

Below: **Baseball games are often held at night.**

Many Americans enjoy watching television, listening to music, or reading. In 1987, the United States had 1,646 newspapers. Magazines include *Reader's Digest, Time, Newsweek* and the *National Geographic*. Popular hobbies include gardening, collecting, computer games and photography.

Many families enjoy outdoor activities, including day or weekend trips to the countryside. The United States has large areas of wilderness which can be enjoyed by hikers. Especially popular are the 49 national parks, which contain much spectacular scenery. The United States led the world in setting up national parks.

Above: **Outdoor activities are popular, especially walking and camping in national parks, such as the beautiful Yosemite National Park in California.**

The arts

The country has produced many great writers including Herman Melville (1819-1891), who wrote *Moby Dick,* and Mark Twain (1855-1910), author of the *Adventures of Huckleberry Finn.*

Leading composers include Aaron Copland (1900-   ) and Leonard Bernstein (1918-   ). The United States has also produced many kinds of popular music. Jazz, which originated among the black people of New Orleans, Louisiana, is a unique American form of music.

Below: **Louis Armstrong (1900-1971) was the best-known of all jazz musicians. He was born in New Orleans, the city that is regarded as the birthplace of jazz.**

The art of film-making was developed largely in the United States. For example, two movies made in the 1910s – *The Birth of a Nation* and *Intolerance* – by the American D.W. Griffith (1875-1948) influenced film-makers worldwide. Today, film-making is a multi-billion dollar industry and Hollywood, the film capital of the world.

Serious drama by such writers as Eugene O'Neill (1888-1953) and Arthur Miller (1915-) have attracted international praise, as also has American ballet. American painters include Charles Marion Russell (1864-1926), who painted Western themes.

Above: **The movie *Raiders of the Lost Ark* (1981) was a huge international success made by the talented film director Steven Spielberg.**

Farming

Only about 4 percent of Americans work in farming, forestry and fishing, as compared with 31 percent in industry. Service industries, such as banking and government, employ the rest. But the United States still leads the world in food production .

Farms, including huge cattle ranches, cover 47 percent of the land. The United States produces more beef, cheese, maize (corn) and soybeans than any other country. Other major crops are potatoes, fruits, cotton, peanuts, rice, sugar, tobacco and wheat. The main cattle ranches are in the Midwest and West. The main dairy cattle regions are in the northeast. The leading producers of wood are the states of Oregon and Washington in the northwest. Fishing is important in both the Atlantic and Pacific oceans.

Below: **Wheat is a major crop in the United States, especially in the Great Plains region.**

Above: **Beef cattle are reared on huge ranches in the western United States.**

Left: **Fishermen mend their nets at Provincetown, Massachusetts.**

Industry

The United States has many other natural resources. It is the world's leading producer of coal and uranium, which is used in nuclear power stations. The country is also the second largest producer of oil and natural gas, after the Soviet Union. About 84 percent of the electricity produced in the United States comes from power stations using coal, oil and natural gas. Nuclear and hydroelectric power stations account for most of the rest.

The country has supplies of most metals and other minerals used in manufacturing. It is among the world's leading producers of asbestos, copper, gold, gypsum, iron ore, lead, phosphate rock, silver and zinc.

Below: **The Grand Coulee Dam, on the Columbia River in the northwest United States, is the country's largest single source of hydroelectricity.**

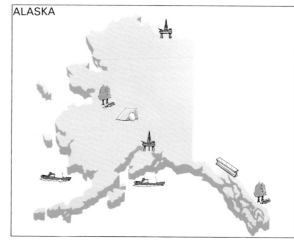

Oil and natural gas		Citrus fruits	
Coal		Peanuts	
Iron ore		Tobacco	
Copper		Forest products	
Industry		Sugar	
Corn (maize)		Pigs	
Wheat		Beef cattle	
Soybeans		Dairy products	
Cotton		Fishing	

Above: **The map shows some of the economic activities in the United States, including the outlying states of Alaska and Hawaii.**

The United States is the world's leading industrial nation. The leading manufacturing states are California, which has many high technology industries, New York, Illinois, Texas, Michigan and Pennsylvania. Major products include vehicles, machinery, armaments, aircraft, electrical and electronic goods, food, chemicals, metal products, printed materials and paper. The United States has developed many industrial techniques, including automation and computerization.

The United States is the world's leading trading country. Its most important trading partners are Canada, Japan, West Germany and Britain.

Below: **This car plant, which uses automated techniques, is in Detroit. Americans call Detroit "the automobile capital of the world".**

Looking to the future

The United States is a rich and powerful nation. Its science and technology have enabled it to become a great industrial power. It has pioneered space exploration, and has put people on the Moon.

The United States is also a major military power and leader of the western countries who are opposed to Communism. The United States has opposed the spread of Communism in several countries, including Korea and Vietnam, where it fought long and very expensive wars.

At home, the United States faces similar problems to other countries. These problems include pollution and unemployment and, especially in the inner cities, crime and drug addiction.

Below: **The United States is a "melting pot" where people of many races and cultures have worked together to create a united, democratic country.**

The United States is seeking to tackle its problems both at home and abroad. For example, the United States and its allies are working with the Soviet Union to ease international differences, reduce the number of weapons held by both sides, and improve chances for world peace.

At home, conservationists have persuaded the government to introduce many laws to protect the environment. The problems of the inner cities are connected with poverty, particularly among minority groups. But most Americans believe that the United States is a land of opportunity, where anyone can become successful and raise their living standards, whatever their race or religion.

Left: **The United States consults its allies when planning its international policies. Here, President George Bush meets the British prime minister, Margaret Thatcher.**

Facts about the United States

Area:
9,370,000 sq km
(3,700,000 sq miles)

Population:
245,800,000

Capital:
Washington D.C.

Largest cities:
New York City (pop
7,284,000)
Los Angeles
(3,342,000)
Chicago (3,018,000)
Houston (1,740,000)

Official language:
English

Religions:
Christianity 87
percent;
Judaism 3 percent

Main exports:
Machinery and
transportation
equipment, other
manufactured goods,
mineral ores and
fuels, chemicals, food
and live animals

Unit of currrency:
US Dollar

United States compared with other countries

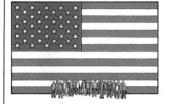

USA 26 per sq km

Britain 232 per sq km

France 100 per sq km

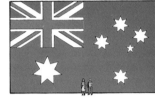

Australia 2 per sq km

Above: **How many people?
The USA is less densely
populated than many
western countries.**

Below: **How large? The
USA is one of the world's
largest countries. It is
bigger than Australia.**

USA

Australia

France UK

Below: **Some money and stamps
used in the United States.**

Arctic Ocean

Brook Range

CANADA

Bering Strait

Yukon R.

Range

△ *Mt McKinley*

Alaska

Anchorage

Seward

Juneau

Kodial I.

eutian Islands

CANADA

L. Superior
Great Lakes
L. Huron

Seattle
Spokane
Portland (Oregon)
Snake R.
Boise

Duluth
L. Michigan
St. Paul
Minneapolis
Milwaukee
Madison
Detroit
L. Erie
Chicago

Portland (Maine
Boston
L. Ontario
Rochester
Buffalo
Cleveland
New York City
Philadelphia
Baltimore
Washington DC

Coast Ranges

Reno
Sacramento
San Francisco
△ *Mt. Whitney*
Great Salt Lake
Great Basin
Salt Lake City
Missouri R.
Great Plains
Omaha
Des Moines
Denver
Lincoln
Kansas City
Indianapolis
Cincinatti
Columbus
Pittsburgh
Mountains
Appalachian
Louisville
Norfolk
Virginia Beach

Las Vegas
Colorado R.
Grand Canyon
Colorado Springs
Wichita
Nashville
Raleigh
Charlotte

Los Angeles
Albuquerque
Tulsa
Memphis
Chattanooga

San Diego
Phoenix
Tucson
Oklahoma City
Red R.
Little Rock
Atlanta
Birmingham
Charleston

El Paso
Fort Worth
Dallas
Shreveport
Mississippi R.
Jackson
Montgomery
Jacksonville

Rio Grande
Austin
Houston
New Orleans
Mobile
Orlando

San Antonio
Tampa
Miami
BAHAMAS

Corpus Christi

Scale 1:10,000,000

0   200   400 km
0 100 200 300 400 miles

Straits of Florida

MEXICO

Gulf of Mexico

CUBA

Kaui
Nihau
Oahu
Honolulu
Lanai
Molokai
Maui
△ *Hilo*
Mauna Loa
Hawaii
Pacific Ocean

JAMAICA

Caribbean Sea

GUATEMALA

BELIZE

HONDURAS

NICARAGUA

Index

PRINTED IN BELGIUM BY

proost
INTERNATIONAL BOOK PRODUCTION